RPM

TRUCKS

The Ins and Outs of *Monster Trucks, Semis, Pickups,* and *Other Trucks*

By Jeff C. Young

Consultants:
Donald Grogg, Executive Director
National Automotive and Truck Museum of the United States
Auburn, Indiana

Paul Keller
Transportation Center for Excellence
Eagan, Minnesota

Ralph Moore, President
Edge-Motorsports

Capstone press®

Mankato, Minnesota

Velocity is published by Capstone Press,
151 Good Counsel Drive, P.O. Box 669, Mankato, Minnesota 56002.
www.capstonepress.com

Books published by Capstone Press are manufactured with paper containing
at least 10 percent post-consumer waste.

Library of Congress Cataloging-in-Publication Data
Young, Jeff C., 1948–
    Trucks : the ins and outs of monster trucks, semis, pickups, and other trucks /
by Jeff C. Young.
        p. cm. — (Velocity — RPM)
    Includes bibliographical references and index.
    Summary: "Describes the details of different types of trucks, including semis,
pickups, monster trucks, work trucks, and service trucks" — Provided by publisher.
    ISBN 978-1-4296-3432-8 (library binding)
    1. Trucks — Juvenile literature. I. Title. II. Series.
TL230.15.Y685 2010
629.224 — dc22   2009003682

Editorial Credits

Carrie Braulick Sheely, editor; Ashlee Suker, designer; Jo Miller, media researcher

Photo Credits

Capstone Press/Karon Dubke, 10, 12, 13, 27 (all), 30, 31, 32, 33, 34 (both), 36–37; Corbis/
Lester Lefkowitz, 38; DEFENSEIMAGERY.MIL/LCPL Matthew J. Anderson, USMC, 41
(top); DEFENSEIMAGERY.MIL/Michelle A. Sosa, 40; Getty Images Inc./Hulton Archive/
Topical Press Agency, 6–7; Getty Images Inc./Photographer's Choice/Lester Lefkowitz,
17; iStockphoto/Jim Parkin, 14–15; iStockphoto/Jonathan Heger, 11; James P. Rowan, 15
(top), 26; Newscom, 29 (inset); Newscom/Icon SMI/Jared C. Tilton, 28–29; Shutterstock/
Aaron Kohr, 16; Shutterstock/Barry Salmons, cover, 4, 21 (top), 25; Shutterstock/Brad
Remy, 45 (top); Shutterstock/Bruce Works, 9 (inset); Shutterstock/David Touchtone, 5;
Shutterstock/felix casio, 22; Shutterstock/Felix Miznioznikov, 20–21; Shutterstock/Henryk
Sadura, 8–9; Shutterstock/Jerry Sharp, 44–45; Shutterstock/Michael Stokes, 18–19;
Shutterstock/Wolfgang Zintl, 39; US Army photo by SGT Jeremiah Johnson, 42–43; US
Marine Corps photo by Lance Cpl. Gene Allen Ainsworth III, 41 (bottom)

Design Elements

Shutterstock/Betacam-SP; Gordan; High Leg Studio; Nicemonkey

The publisher does not endorse products whose logos may appear in images in this book.

Capstone Press dedicates this book to the memory of George Eisenhart, Jr., who assisted
us with the publication of this book by sharing his valuable monster truck expertise.

TABLE OF CONTENTS

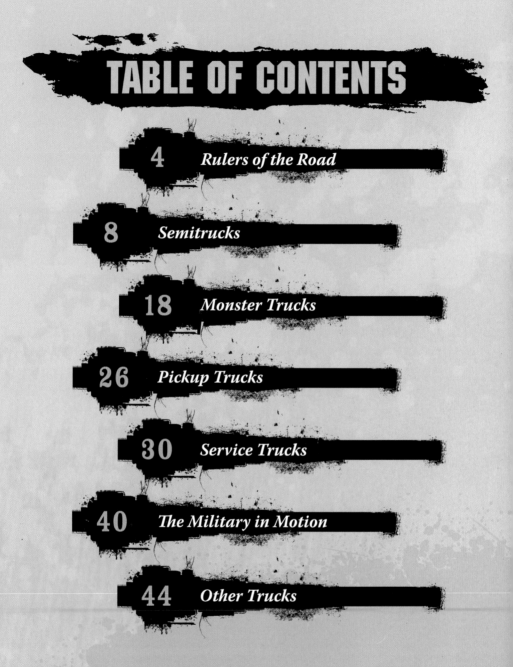

4   *Rulers of the Road*

8   *Semitrucks*

18   *Monster Trucks*

26   *Pickup Trucks*

30   *Service Trucks*

40   *The Military in Motion*

44   *Other Trucks*

Glossary *46*

Read More *47*

Internet Sites *47*

Index *48*

RULERS OF THE ROAD

In a world without trucks, store shelves and gas pumps would be empty. Garbage would pile up in the streets. Wrecked cars wouldn't be moved, and huge snowdrifts would block highways. This book wouldn't even be in your hands!

Maybe you haven't thought about it much before, but trucks play a role in many parts of your life. Trucks deliver almost everything that you use on a daily basis. They haul your family's camping gear up steep winding gravel roads. They remove your garbage, deliver packages, and help put out fires.

And don't forget entertainment. Zipping
around a racetrack and crunching junked cars are
just two ways trucks draw millions of fans to their
action-packed events.

TIME LINE OF THE TRUCKING INDUSTRY

1895 The Daimler-Motoren-Gesellschaft company produces the first truck line in Germany. The line has trucks with four-, six-, eight-, or 10-horsepower engines.

1898 The U.S.-based Winton company builds a delivery truck powered by a gasoline six-horsepower engine.

1900 Trucks are used to transport goods in Europe and the United States. Some early trucks carry loads weighing up to 5 tons (4.5 metric tons).

1907 Chicago, Illinois, hosts one of the first major U.S. truck shows.

1914–1918 Trucks transport weapons and supplies during World War I.

1915 The number of trucks in the United States skyrockets to more than 150,000.

1916 The Federal Aid Road Act of 1916 passes. It funds the building of paved highways that connect major U.S. cities.

1939–1945 During World War II, trucks again play a major role in transporting supplies to battlefields.

1956 The U.S. Congress passes a law that establishes the current system of interstate highways. The interstate highways allow bigger and faster trucks to move goods across the country.

Argyll truck, 1907

1986 U.S. Congress passes the Commercial Motor Vehicle Safety Act. The law requires states to test and license semitruck drivers.

2006 Truck drivers hold about 2.9 million jobs in the United States.

SEMITRUCKS

The trucks that crisscross our highways delivering goods have a variety of names. They're known as big rigs, heavy trucks, 18-wheelers, tractor-trailers, and semitrucks. Most of the time, though, they're just called semis. Semis are the biggest and heaviest trucks on our highways. Along with store goods, semis transport logs, fuel, cattle, and oversized cargo like houses.

Tractor: The front of the semi is called the tractor. Like a farm tractor, it pulls a load behind it. The tractor houses the engine and the cab where the driver sits. A tractor without its trailer is sometimes called a "bobtail."

Tractor Front Axles: In North America, most semi tractors have three axles. The front axle has two wheels. It is also known as the steer axle.

Fifth Wheel: The back of a tractor has a device called a fifth wheel. The fifth wheel locks the trailer into place.

Trailer Axles: The trailer usually has two rear axles. Each axle has two wheels on each side. Most trailers, then, ride on eight wheels.

Tractor Back Axles: The back of the tractor has two rear-drive axles. The rear axles usually have two tires on each side.

THE POWER BEHIND THE PULL

The engine size of a semi varies depending on its weight and its use. Most semi engines are V-8s. The number "8" stands for the number of cylinders the engine has. Fuel burns inside the cylinders. Engines with a higher number of cylinders produce more power than engines with fewer cylinders.

Semi engines burn diesel fuel. Engines that run on diesel fuel last longer and burn fuel more efficiently than gasoline-powered engines do.

Most semi engines produce at least 500 horsepower. That's about double the amount of power that a standard passenger car produces.

Car Engine Life:
  About 200,000 miles (321,870 km)

Semi Engine Life:
  About 1,000,000 miles (1,609,344 km)

Items like milk, cheese, fruit, and vegetables spoil in temperatures above 40 degrees Fahrenheit (4 degrees Celsius). That's why they travel in refrigerated trucks. The trailer is insulated to help maintain the cool temperature inside. Once the trailer is loaded, the doors stay tightly locked until the truck is unloaded. A thermometer on the trailer's side allows the driver to check the temperature without opening the trailer.

Before refrigerated trucks, food was ice-cooled. But the food spoiled when the ice melted too quickly. In the mid-1930s, engineer Frederick McKinley Jones invented a small refrigeration unit that could withstand the bumps of long-distance deliveries. At first, the unit was mounted under the truck. But it would stop working when it got clogged with mud. The unit was then moved to the front of the truck above the cab.

truck air-conditioning unit

A HOME ON WHEELS

Drivers who spend days at a time in their trucks delivering goods are called "over-the-road" drivers. Their cabs, called "condos," let them enjoy some comforts of home. Condos have a sleeping area in the back. They often have appliances like microwaves and refrigerators. Some condos also have bathrooms, TVs, and video game consoles.

The U.S. government sometimes hires truck drivers to deliver top secret cargo or dangerous weapons. The drivers hired for these jobs have very good driving records and a great deal of experience behind the wheel.

The first step to becoming a semi driver is to earn a commercial driver's license (CDL). All applicants must pass the general knowledge written test. Drivers also take other written tests based on what type of truck they want to drive. These tests may include:

- hazardous materials
- doubles and triples, for drivers pulling two or three trailers
- air brakes
- tankers

Applicants also must pass a driving test. Many drivers earn their CDL after taking classes offered by private schools.

Federal rules limit drivers to working no more than 70 hours in an eight-day period. Also, after a driver has driven for 11 hours, he or she must have 10 hours off before driving again. Most drivers are required to track their driving time in a log book. A typical driver covers 550 to 650 miles (885 to 1,046 kilometers) in a day.

LOGGING TRUCKS

There are two types of logging trucks — on-highway and off-highway. On-highway trucks are allowed on public highways. But they have to follow restrictions set by federal and state governments. The bigger, heavier off-highway trucks don't have to follow these rules. The most powerful logging trucks can haul three or more trailers at once.

Gross Weight
80,000 lb
(36,287 kg)

The trailer of a logging truck is a long, flat platform called a flatbed. The sides of the flatbed have long, upright brackets to keep the logs from rolling off.

Length
60 ft (18 m) maximum

The United States, Canada, New Zealand, Norway, Finland, and Sweden are all big users of logging trucks. Swedish manufacturers Scania and Volvo are especially well known for their high-powered logging trucks.

Height
13.5 ft (4 m) maximum

Width
8.5 ft (2.6 m) maximum

TANKERS

Tankers haul large loads of liquids or powders. Common tanker cargo includes gasoline, hazardous chemicals, and milk. Early tankers of the 1920s had rectangular tanks. Later on, tanks shaped like cylinders became the norm.

Some tanks have six or more separate compartments. These sections are needed when the cargo has types or grades. For example, a gasoline tanker needs to keep the different types of gasoline separated.

Tank design depends on the cargo. Insulated tanks help keep cargo at a steady temperature. Stainless steel tanks often carry food because they are easy to clean.

Tanks can be filled from the top or the bottom. A top-loading tanker often has a ladder attached to the tank and a walkway on its top.

A tanker's contents are either pumped out or emptied by gravity, like when you pull out the plug of a sink.

MONSTER TRUCKS

Like Dr. Frankenstein in the famous book *Frankenstein*, Bob Chandler created a monster. But instead of a humanlike monster, he created a monster truck that he called Bigfoot.

In the mid-1970s, four-wheel-drive (4X4) pickup trucks were popular. Chandler's garage in Hazelwood, Missouri, fixed and customized 4X4 trucks. Chandler had a limited advertising budget, so he turned his own truck into a billboard on wheels.

Over time, Chandler further customized his Ford F-250 pickup. He added huge 48-inch (122-centimeter) tires, a more powerful engine, and a stronger suspension. Soon, curious people were driving by Chandler's garage just to look at Bigfoot. The truck attracted so much attention that Chandler decided to take Bigfoot on the road.

By 1979, Bigfoot was appearing at car shows throughout the United States. In 1981, Chandler made a video of Bigfoot crushing a row of junked cars. That same year, Bigfoot was shown in a popular movie.

Soon, other people built trucks like Bigfoot. The oversize trucks made appearances at mud races and truck pulls. There was no denying it — monster truck mania had begun.

Since Bob Chandler created the first Bigfoot, he and his crew have built 15 other monster trucks with the Bigfoot name.

In 1984, the first monster truck show was held at the Silverdome in Michigan. Two years later, the first monster truck race thrilled fans at the Astrodome in Houston, Texas.

Height of truck jump = about 15 ft (4.6 m)

Today, monster truck shows are held across the United States and Europe. Shows feature races, donut competitions, wheelie competitions, and other events.

The popular Monster Jam shows bring fans to their feet in every corner of the United States. Each season ends with the Monster Jam World Finals in Las Vegas, Nevada.

In wheelie competitions, drivers perform their best wheelies. The tallest wheelies are called sky wheelies because the truck stands nearly straight up in the air!

The longest monster truck wheelie ever recorded was 217 feet, 3 inches (66 meters, 22 centimeters). Bigfoot 11 set this record in 1999.

Length of monster truck stadium jump = up to 100 ft (30 m)

A MONSTER DESIGN

Tires: The oversize tires are normally found on earthmoving equipment. Most tires are 66 inches (168 centimeters) tall and 3.5 feet (1 meter) wide. A new set of tires costs around $7,200.

Body: A monster truck's body is made of fiberglass. Fiberglass is lighter and easier to repair than metal.

Rims: The strong steel rims can withstand the force of 5 tons (4.5 metric tons) pressing down on them.

Engine: A powerful engine is mounted behind the driver. Most engines produce about 1,500 horsepower, but some produce up to 2,000 horsepower. Monster truck engines run on methanol. An engine burning this alcohol-based fuel produces more power than a gasoline-powered engine.

Frame: A monster truck's frame is made of lightweight steel tubes. It is about 12 feet (3.7 meters) wide.

Axles: Heavy-duty axles come from other vehicles like school buses, military trucks, or tractors.

STAYING SAFE

Along with creating the first monster truck, Bob Chandler helped form the Monster Truck Racing Association (MTRA). In 1987, Chandler invited other monster truck owners to write guidelines for monster truck racing. Their major goals were increasing driver and spectator safety and promoting the sport.

Today, all MTRA-sanctioned trucks must pass a yearly safety and mechanical inspection. Drivers also have to get certified. After taking classroom training, drivers earn a class-B MTRA license. This license is like a learner's permit. A class-B driver must compete in 10 monster truck shows under the supervision of a class-A-rated driver. Afterward, the class B license can be upgraded to class A.

All MTRA-certified drivers must wear a fire-resistant suit, helmet, safety harness, neck collar, and gloves.

Monster truck races include obstacles such as ramps and rows of junked cars.

A remote ignition interrupter allows a show official to shut off the monster truck's engine by remote control. It's used in case the driver loses control of the truck.

MTRA-sanctioned trucks have a steel roll cage that protects the driver in a rollover.

PICKUP TRUCKS

Before pickups, the only trucks on the road were huge work trucks. Farmers and construction workers wanted smaller trucks. Their jobs required them to have an affordable vehicle for hauling tools and supplies.

REO Speedwagon, International Harvester, Ford, and other manufacturers made some of the first pickups in the early 1900s. Called "light duty trucks," they came with a flatbed instead of a fully enclosed bed. In 1925, Ford released the popular Model T Runabout. With its steel bed, the truck had a more modern design.

Before manufacturers built pickups with beds, owners added their own.

In the late 1950s, Ford and Chevrolet experimented by attaching beds to car frames. In 1957, Ford introduced the Ranchero. This car had a 6-foot (1.8-meter) cargo bed. Two years later, Chevrolet made the El Camino. It had a double-wall pickup bed on a car frame.

1,850-pound (839-kilogram) maximum payload

cargo management system

2009 Dodge Ram

integrated bed divider/extender

Today's pickups have come a long way from their early days. From mega-hauling power to handy built-in tool boxes, modern pickups are made to get the job done.

rear-view camera

2009 Ford F-150

tailgate step

27

Pickup trucks may be practical, but that doesn't mean they can't fly around a racetrack. In 1993, off-road truck racers built pickups for racing on pavement. They showed off their vehicles at the 1994 Daytona 500 NASCAR race. Fans loved them instantly, so NASCAR created a racing series just for trucks in 1995. Craftsman Tools became a major sponsor, and the NASCAR Craftsman Truck Series was created in 1996. In 2009, the name of the series changed to the NASCAR Camping World Truck Series.

There are strict rules for the trucks racing on the NASCAR circuit. Trucks must:

√ weigh at least 3,500 pounds (1,588 kilograms) with a full fuel tank.

√ have a four-speed manual transmission.

√ have a wheelbase of 112 inches (284 centimeters).

√ use 98 octane unleaded fuel.

Greg Biffle was the first driver in the Craftsman Truck Series to earn more than $1 million in one year. In 2002, he earned $1,002,510.

Some NASCAR stock car drivers race NASCAR trucks as well. These drivers include Kevin Harvick and Kyle Bush.

SERVICE TRUCKS

Is your garbage piling up? Need a tow after a fender bender? When you need a helping hand, service trucks won't let you down.

GARBAGE TRUCKS

As the world's population grows, people are producing more garbage. Over time, bigger garbage trucks were built to handle all the trash. Some of today's garbage trucks weigh more than 30 tons (27 metric tons). The huge trucks can have three or four axles.

In the mid-1700s, cities in the United States and Europe had no organized way of collecting garbage. People piled garbage outside their doors or dumped it out their windows. In Scotland, people even yelled out a warning before throwing waste out the window. Then others underneath them could get out of the way!

When the truck gets full, a packing panel smashes the waste to create more room in the hopper.

Mechanical arms lift dumpsters and trash bins. They then empty the contents into the truck's hopper.

TOW TRUCKS

Stranded motorists are usually relieved to see a tow truck headed their way. But not everyone gets towed because they want to. Vehicles are also towed after they've been wrecked or illegally parked.

Boom: Tow trucks have a long metal arm called a boom. Operators use the boom when they cannot safely back up to a vehicle. The boom pulls the vehicle closer to the truck. At least one hook on a long cable is attached to the boom. A motor-driven machine called a winch winds and unwinds the cable.

Wheel Lift: Most tow trucks use a tire or wheel lift. The lift uses brackets that are held in place by steel pins. After the device lifts the vehicle, the front or rear wheels are cradled by the brackets. The wheel lift leaves the vehicle undamaged because it only touches the tires. An experienced operator can secure the wheels in less than 30 seconds.

FLATBED TOW TRUCKS

A winch and cable are also used on flatbed tow trucks. Flatbeds are used when a vehicle is too heavy or too damaged to be towed by a regular tow truck. A hydraulic system lowers the bed to the ground. The cable then pulls the vehicle onto the flatbed.

UP, UP, AND AWAY!

An integrated wheel lift, or self-loading wheel lift, is one of the most advanced tow truck devices. It allows the operator to hook up a vehicle without leaving the cab.

tow truck with integrated wheel lift

integrated wheel lift cab controls

In most car and truck purchases, the buyer borrows money to pay for the vehicle. Generally, the money is borrowed from a bank. The borrower agrees to make regular payments until the loan is repaid. If the borrower fails to make the payments, the bank often decides to take the vehicle back. That's when repossession, or "repo," workers spring into action.

Repo workers try to do their jobs when the borrower is sleeping or away from home. That helps them avoid an argument with the borrower.

1. The operator backs up the tow truck.

2. Controls in the cab are used to lower the wheel lift behind the truck. The lift attaches the brackets to the vehicle's wheels using hydraulics.

3. The operator raises the wheel lift and the vehicle. In a matter of seconds, the operator is ready to drive off.

A reality TV show called *Operation Repo* gives viewers an inside look at a repo business' daily activities.

FIRE TRUCKS

Usually you hear a fire truck before you see it. The wailing of its siren warns motorists to get out of the way.

Fire truck design varies depending on the truck's use. Trucks that pump water onto a fire are called "pumpers." Other trucks carry rescue equipment. Ladder trucks raise tall ladders so firefighters can battle fires on the upper levels of buildings.

Nozzles on the bucket shoot out water.

Buckets support firefighters. A bucket may hold up to seven fighters.

Tanker trucks can carry more than 1,000 gallons (3,785 liters) of water. If the water is needed, firefighters empty the water into a large container that looks like a swimming pool. A pumper truck can then pump water from the container.

Ladders can reach more than 100 feet (30 meters) high.

ladder truck

Extra side doors allow firefighters to reach equipment easily and quickly.

Many fire trucks hold foam as well as water. Firefighters often spray foam onto fuel fires. The foam has special materials in it to put out fuel fires quickly.

DUMP TRUCKS

You may not see them, but dump trucks are hard at work every day. Standard dump trucks have a cargo area that is attached to the truck's frame. Hydraulic equipment dumps the loads after the driver presses a button in the cab.

The largest dump trucks work in mines and gravel pits. Also called haul trucks, they carry several tons of rock and dirt from place to place. Because they are so big and heavy, mining trucks aren't used on highways.

In 2008, the world's largest truck was the Liebherr T282B dump truck. This mining truck can carry a 400-ton (363-metric-ton) load. The gigantic machine is powered by a 3,650-horsepower engine. The engine guzzles 50 gallons (189 liters) of diesel fuel in one hour. The truck's designer, Francis Bartley, said operating the truck was "like driving a house."

LET IT SNOW!

If you live in a cold climate, you've probably seen snowplows. These big trucks have huge plows attached to their front ends. Flashing lights warn motorists of a snowplow's presence. Some snowplows haul gravel and push snow. They dump out the gravel onto roadways to give cars better traction on slick roads.

THE MILITARY IN MOTION

Without trucks, a modern military couldn't fight a battle. Military trucks bring food, weapons, medical supplies, and everything else that an army needs.

ONE TRUCK, MANY JOBS

The HMMWV is one of the most useful military trucks. The truck's initials stand for High-Mobility Multipurpose Wheeled Vehicle, but it is more commonly called a "Humvee." The Humvee has several different models. They include:

M997 AMBULANCE

- Holds four stretchers
- Carries eight patients without stretchers
- Equipped with armor
- Can be heated, ventilated, or air-conditioned

M1042 SHELTER CARRIER

- Carries S250 electrical equipment shelter
- Has payload of 3,600 pounds (1,633 kilograms)
- Equipped with armor
- Has winch to recover other vehicles

The weapons platform turns in a full circle.

WEAPONS CARRIERS

Can carry:

- TOW missile system
- M2 .50-caliber machine gun
- MK-19 Automatic Grenade Launcher
- M60 7.62 mm machine gun

HEMTT

The HEMTT's initials stand for Heavy Expanded Mobility Tactical Truck. It carries up to 11 tons (10 metric tons) of cargo. There are five different models. Two of the models are cargo carriers. Two other models serve as a fuel truck and a tow truck. A fifth model pulls a trailer used to launch missiles.

The HEMTT has a Load Handling System (LHS). The LHS helps the truck load and unload cargo.

Since the early 2000s, the U.S. Army has been interested in using vehicles that run on hybrid power. Hybrid vehicles have engines that run on both electricity and either gasoline or diesel fuel. They are more fuel-efficient than vehicles that run only on diesel or gasoline. Because it produces less heat, a hybrid engine can also help keep enemy heat sensors from noticing the vehicle. The Army plans to use hybrid power for its FCS (Future Combat Systems) vehicles after testing is complete. The first vehicles may roll onto battlefields as early as 2011.

The HEMTT's cargo sits on beds called flatracks.

OTHER TRUCKS

A few die-hard truck fans have taken their love of trucks to new heights. Some truck owners have customized their trucks to do wheelies. Others race semi tractors on paved tracks built for stock car racing. Truck owners may also compete in drag races. In these races, two drivers speed side by side down a paved track. The winner is the first driver across the finish line. All of these truck owners prove that a truck's design and use is limited only by one's imagination.

JET TRUCKS

Jet trucks are built to break speed records. These trucks use engines made for jet planes. A jet truck called Shockwave holds the world record for the highest full-size truck speed. How fast did it go to break this record? An amazing 376 miles (605 kilometers) per hour!

Lowrider trucks have bodies that just sit above the road.

GLOSSARY

axle (AK-suhl) — a rod in the center of a wheel around which the wheel turns

cargo (KAHR-goh) — goods carried by a truck, ship, or aircraft

customize (KUHS-tuh-myz) — to change a vehicle according to the owner's needs and tastes

cylinder (SI-luhn-duhr) — a hollow area inside an engine in which fuel burns to create power

efficient (uh-FI-shuhnt) — not wasteful of time or energy

fiberglass (FY-buhr-glas) — a strong, lightweight material made from thin threads of glass

horsepower (HORSS-pou-ur) — a unit for measuring an engine's power

hybrid (HY-brid) — a mix of two different types; hybrid engines run on electricity and gasoline or diesel fuel.

hydraulic (hye-DRAW-lik) — having to do with a system powered by fluid forced through pipes or chambers

permit (PUR-mit) — a written statement giving permission for something

restriction (ri-STRIK-shun) — a rule or limitation

sanction (SANGK-shuhn) — to allow or give approval

stock car (STOK CAR) — a car built for racing on paved tracks that is based on the regular model sold to the public

traction (TRAK-shuhn) — the gripping power that holds a vehicle's tires to the ground

46

Graham, Ian. *Trucks and Earthmovers.* The World's Greatest. Chicago: Raintree, 2006.

Mattern, Joanne. *Track Trucks!* Stock Car Racing. New York: Children's Press, 2007.

Morganelli, Adrianna. *Trucks: Pickups to Big Rigs*. Automania! New York: Crabtree, 2007.

INTERNET SITES

FactHound offers a safe, fun way to find Internet sites related to this book. All of the sites on FactHound have been researched by our staff.

Here's all you do:

Visit *www.facthound.com*

FactHound will fetch the best sites for you!

INDEX

axles, 8, 9, 23, 30

Biffle, Greg, 29
Bigfoot, 18–19, 21

Chandler, Bob, 18–19, 24
condos, 12
cylinders (of engines), 10

diesel fuel, 10, 38, 43
drivers, 7, 8, 11, 12, 13, 23, 24, 25, 29, 38, 44
dump trucks, 38
    Liebherr T282B, 38

El Camino, 26
engines, 6, 8, 10, 18, 23, 25, 38, 43

fifth wheel, 9
fire trucks, 36–37
flatbed trailers, 14, 26, 33
frames, 23, 26, 38

garbage trucks, 4, 30–31

HEMTTs, 42–43
HMMWVs. See Humvees
Humvees, 40–41
hybrid vehicles, 43

integrated wheel lift, 34-35

jet trucks, 44

lowrider trucks, 45

Monster Truck Racing Association (MTRA), 24–25
monster trucks, 18–25
    shows, 20–21, 24–25

NASCAR Camping World Truck Series, 28–29

pickups, 26–29

Ranchero, 26

self-loading wheel lift. See integrated wheel lift
semitrucks, 7, 8–17, 44
    logging trucks, 14–15
    tankers, 16–17
snowplows, 39

tires, 9, 18, 22, 32
tow trucks, 32–35, 42